Contents

Any words appearing in the text in bold, **like this**, are explained in the Glossary.

What is energy?

Do you know what these all have in common:

● launching a rocket into space

● running a marathon

● lighting a city at night

● drilling for oil under the oceans?

The answer is simple: they all use energy. All your activities also use energy. Everything you do, from cleaning your teeth to playing football, from eating a meal to playing tennis, from reading a book to riding a bicycle, uses energy. Some things use a lot of energy, while others use very little. Some things provide energy for us to use. But have you ever stopped to think about what the word "energy" really means?

This book tells you about the brilliant scientists who unravelled the many mysteries of energy, and the inventors who developed new ways of obtaining energy. It follows the amazing chain of discoveries, from the earliest forms of energy generation in ancient times to the scientific breakthroughs that are still being made today. Together, all these links in the chain have brought about many of the things that we now take for granted in our everyday lives.

WHO GAVE ENERGY ITS NAME?

We now use the word energy to mean "the ability to do work or make something happen". The word energy was first used in this sense in 1807, by an English scientist called Thomas Young (1773–1829). It comes from the Greek word *energeia*, which is made up of two Greek words (*en* which means "in" and *ergon* which means "work"). Thomas Young was a very hard-working and well-educated man. As well as working as a doctor and carrying out his scientific studies, he also solved some of the mysteries of ancient Egyptian hieroglyphics.

We know that energy can exist in many forms. Four are probably familiar to you: heat, light, sound, and electricity. Others are:

- chemical energy, which is the energy stored in chemicals

- nuclear energy, which is the energy stored inside atoms

- potential energy, which is the energy stored in something because of its position

- **kinetic energy**, which is the energy of anything that is moving.

In the past, these types of energy were all thought to be very different. But we now know that they are all just different forms of the same thing. We also know that one form of energy can be changed into another. For example, in a car engine the chemical energy stored in the petrol is changed into light, heat, sound, and kinetic energy.

These are some of the many different forms of energy.

kinetic energy
of wind

chemical
energy in fuels

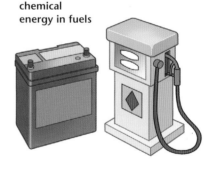

potential energy at the
top of a waterfall

nuclear energy
in an atom

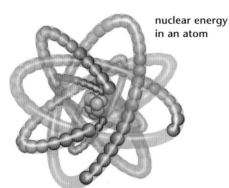

Sources of energy

The most important source of heat and light energy on Earth is the Sun. Without the Sun, our planet would be cold, dark, and dead. The Sun's light and heat are vital for plants and animals to live. But the Sun does not stop the winters being cold and the nights being dark.

Since prehistoric times, people have used fire as an extra source of heat and light. To fuel their fires, the earliest peoples used natural sources of energy that they found in the world around them. The most common fuel was wood, although there is also evidence of dried animal dung being burned. Stone hearths from archaeological excavations show that humans were using fire earlier than 750,000 BC. By around 79,000 BC, animal fat was being used in simple stone lamps, with grass or moss as a wick. Wood, animal dung, and animal fat all contain chemical energy. These stores of chemical energy turn into heat and light energy when they are burned.

A wood fire provides both heat and light energy.

Later on, kinetic energy was also harnessed. Wind is moving air, and therefore has kinetic energy. This form of energy can push against the sails of boats, propelling them through water. Sailing boats existed in Mesopotamia as early as 4000 BC. The wind's energy was also used to turn the sails of windmills, which in turn drove the machinery inside the mill. The first known windmill was built in Persia in the mid-7th century AD.

HOW CAN ANIMALS PROVIDE ENERGY?

For thousands of years, people have used the energy of animals to do work. Horses, bullocks, yaks, and other strong animals could be used to plough land and pull carts. Later, they were used to turn wheels to drive machinery.

For centuries, animals have provided farmers with a source of energy. These oxen are being used to plough a paddy field in Cambodia.

The kinetic energy of moving water from rivers and waterfalls was used to turn the wheels of water mills. The wheels then drove the machinery inside the mills. The first recorded water mill was constructed in France, at the beginning of the 13th century.

As people came to understand more about scientific principles and the world around them, they developed more complex machines. During the **Industrial Revolution** in the 18th century, machinery began to be used to manufacture cloth and other goods on a larger scale. This required more fuel, such as coal. To provide coal, more mines were needed. Larger-scale manufacturing also required better transport, to move goods from place to place. The 18th-century expansion of industry therefore led to an increasing demand for energy.

The power of steam

One problem for the early coalmining industry was the fact that many mines were easily flooded. This was dangerous for the miners working under ground. It also made the mining process slower. The water could be removed using a system of buckets and pulleys operated by horses, but this was expensive and slow. A better solution was required. The answer came in 1698 when an English scientist, Thomas Savery (c.1650–1715), **patented** the first workable steam engine. But this was only possible because of the work of earlier scientists on **vacuums**.

A vacuum is a space that contains absolutely nothing. Since the time of the ancient Greek philosopher and scientist Aristotle (384–322 BC), people had believed that it was impossible for a vacuum to exist in nature.

Scientists found that they could create a vacuum using a pump made from a movable cylinder inside a tight-fitting tube. However, this vacuum was extremely weak and lasted only a short time.

HERO OF ALEXANDRIA'S STORY

This is the steam device invented by Hero of Alexandria in around AD 62.

Hero of Alexandria was a 1st-century Greek scientist who developed a rotating device that was known as an aeolipile. A large, sealed vessel containing water, with a closed lid, was placed over a fire. Two pipes came out of the top of the vessel, and a ball was suspended between them. The fire heated the water until it boiled and turned into steam. As the steam rushed out of the pipes, it made the ball spin round very fast. This was the first recorded use of steam to make something move, but it was only used as an amusing toy!

In the mid-17th century an Italian scientist, Evangelista Torricelli (1608–1647), investigated this further. In 1643, he proved that it was possible to create a satisfactory vacuum. A few years later, in the 1650s, a German scientist called Otto von Guericke (1602–1686) developed an air pump that could create a much stronger vacuum.

In 1690, a French scientist called Denis Papin (1647–1712) proved it was possible to use steam to move a **piston**. A piston is a cylinder that is encased in a tight-fitting tube. By cooling the steam, a partial vacuum is created, and this moves the piston. Using steam to move a piston was an important step forward, because the movement of the piston could be used to move other parts of a machine.

From these beginnings came Thomas Savery's steam pump. He called it "The Miners' Friend", because he had designed it specifically for pumping water out of coalmines. Two large boilers heated water until it evaporated into steam. Filling one large container with steam and then cooling it created a vacuum. This vacuum drew water up from the mine via a series of pipes. Steam from the boilers could then force the water out completely.

This illustration shows Thomas Savery's steam pump, patented in 1698. Most mines proved to be too deep for the machine to be effective. However, it was used to supply water to country houses and estates.

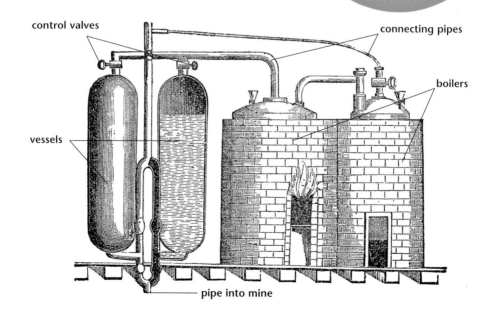

control valves

connecting pipes

boilers

vessels

pipe into mine

Improving steam engines

Thomas Savery's steam engine was a definite improvement on the use of horses, buckets, and pulleys, but it was not perfect. It had to be within about 7.5 metres (25 feet) of the water. It was also dangerous: because steam was at high **pressure** and there were no safety valves, the boilers and the large vessels could easily explode!

Another Englishman, called Thomas Newcomen (1663–1729), improved Savery's steam engine by using a central beam that rocked up and down. This action drove a pump, which pumped water out of the mines. In 1712, Newcomen demonstrated the power of his engine by pumping water out of a flooded mine. News of the invention spread quickly. Soon, Newcomen engines were installed at mines throughout England and Wales.

This is a model of a steam engine, designed by Thomas Newcomen and known as a beam engine.

A Scottish engineer, James Watt (1736–1839), and his partner Matthew Boulton (1728–1809), developed Newcomen's design even further. By 1775, their engines were much more efficient than Newcomen's, using less energy to do the same amount of work.

Watt and Boulton then developed a steam engine that could be used to power other machinery. It had a **flywheel** that could be driven by the beam, via a set of gears. Its speed was controlled by a device called a "governor". These steam engines became popular with manufacturers, who wanted them to drive machinery in their mills and factories. This invention was one of the factors that made the 18th-century **Industrial Revolution** possible.

The first steam train

The first steam locomotive was built in 1804 by an engineer called Richard Trevithick (1771–1833). It ran on the rails that had, until then, been used for horse-drawn trucks at an ironworks in Penydarren, in Wales. Unfortunately, the rails were not strong enough to carry the weight of the locomotive, and the idea was abandoned. Trevithick did not give up, though. In 1808, he built a circular track in Euston Square, London. He ran a steam locomotive around it, which he called "Catch-me-if-you-can". It was very popular and many people queued for a ride.

THAT'S AMAZING!

By 1829, George Stephenson's *Rocket* could pull a train at a speed of 48 kilometres (30 miles) per hour. This was a great improvement on the 8 kilometres (5 miles) per hour of the early models.

Other engineers developed Trevithick's locomotive, and improved the design of the rails. In 1825, the Stockton & Darlington Railway opened. This was the first public railway to use steam locomotives. Railways soon opened all over Britain, and locomotive design rapidly improved.

Railway technology spread to places far from Britain, such as India and Russia. In the United States, long railroads helped pioneers to move further west. The first US transcontinental line was opened in 1869.

Ideas about steam and thermodynamics

While engineers were building and improving steam engines, scientists were asking questions such as "What is steam?" and "How and why do steam engines work?" Their increasing understanding of steam led to the development of the science known as **thermodynamics**.

This engraving shows Robert Boyle (on the right) with the French chemist Denis Papin (left), who assisted Boyle with some of his research.

In the early steam engines, coal provided the energy needed to heat the water. But only about 3 per cent of the energy provided by the fuel was converted into mechanical work. Engineers tried to reduce the amount of wasted energy. However, in order to increase the efficiency of the engines, they needed to find out more about gases and liquids.

In the 1660s, an Irish scientist called Robert Boyle (1627–1691) found that a gas takes up much more space than a liquid of the same weight. If the gas is compressed into a smaller space than it naturally takes up, it pushes back with a force called pressure. Robert Boyle worked out the relationship between the **volume** of a gas (the amount of space it takes up) and the amount of pressure it exerts. According to Boyle's law, the more the gas is compressed, the greater the pressure it exerts.

Over 100 years later, in 1787, a French scientist called Jacques Alexandre César Charles (1746–1823) developed this idea even further. By testing different gases, he found out that, for a given rise in temperature, every gas expands the same amount. This became known as Charles's law.

This illustration shows the three states of water, depending on its temperature and pressure: solid (ice), liquid (water), and gas (vapour).

Water is a useful substance for scientific investigations because it can exist as a solid, a liquid, or a gas at normal temperatures. At temperatures between 0 °Celsius (32 °Fahrenheit) and 100 °Celsius (212 °Fahrenheit), water is a liquid. Its **molecules** are loosely bound together. The liquid can flow and change its shape, but it cannot change its volume. At 100 °Celsius (212 °Fahrenheit), liquid water **evaporates** and turns to water vapour. Its molecules are no longer bound together. The gas can flow and change its shape, and it can also change its volume. If the temperature falls below 100 °Celsius (212 °Fahrenheit), its molecules become loosely bound together again, and the water vapour **condenses** back into liquid water.

IS STEAM THE SAME AS WATER VAPOUR?

Although people often talk about water vapour and steam as if they are identical, they are not. Steam is a hot, visible mixture of airborne water droplets and water vapour, while water vapour is invisible and can exist at any temperature above 0 °Celsius (32 °Fahrenheit).

Discovering electricity

While some scientists and engineers were exploring the science of energy and steam, others were investigating static electricity. The existence of static electricity was known to people several thousand years ago, although nobody could explain what caused it, or why.

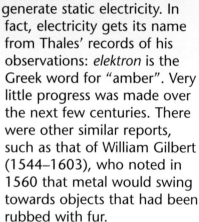

Amber is the fossilized resin of pine trees. It is often used to make beads for necklaces.

Thales (c.624–c.548 BC), an ancient Greek philosopher, found that rubbing a piece of amber with a silk cloth or a piece of fur could generate static electricity. In fact, electricity gets its name from Thales' records of his observations: *elektron* is the Greek word for "amber". Very little progress was made over the next few centuries. There were other similar reports, such as that of William Gilbert (1544–1603), who noted in 1560 that metal would swing towards objects that had been rubbed with fur.

In 1733, a French scientist, Charles Dufay (1698–1739), proved that there were two different types of electric charge. Rubbing sealing wax with wool produced one type of charge. Rubbing glass with silk produced another type of electric charge. Dufay also found that similar charges repelled (pushed away from each other), while different charges were attracted to each other. If the two different charges were put together, they seemed to cancel each other out. Although Dufay's observations were accurate, his suggestion that static electricity was created from two fluids was later found to be incorrect.

Benjamin Franklin's experiments

In the United States, Benjamin Franklin (1706–1790) was also investigating static electricity. Like Dufay, he thought that materials contained an electrical "fluid". Unlike Dufay, though, Franklin thought there was just a single fluid. He decided that, when two materials were rubbed together, part of the fluid moved from one of the materials to the other. The effect of this was to unbalance the materials. One lost something, while the other gained something. Franklin decided that the loser had a "negative charge" while the gainer had a "positive charge".

Benjamin Franklin, the famous American statesman, printer, and scientist, invented several things, including the lightning conductor and bifocal spectacles.

Benjamin Franklin also thought that lightning was really static electricity. In 1752, he carried out a dangerous experiment with a kite during a thunderstorm. Franklin attached a piece of metal wire to the kite end of the string and a metal key to the lower end of the string. The lightning was attracted to the metal wire, which was a good **conductor** of electricity. The lightning then flowed down the kite string, causing the key at the bottom to spark when he touched it. This proved that lightning really was a form of electricity.

? HOW DO LIGHTNING CONDUCTORS WORK?

Metal lightning conductors are commonly placed on the roofs of buildings to protect them from damage. Being made of metal, a lightning conductor offers the best path for the electricity to flow to the ground without damaging the building.

Storing electricity

As interest in electrical energy grew, scientists began to wonder if there was a way of storing it so that a steady flow of electricity could be produced. The first step was taken in 1663. The German scientist Otto von Guericke invented a very simple instrument to generate static electricity. His "generator" provided a way of charging a rotating ball of sulphur with static electricity. When von Guericke touched the ball, sparks were given off.

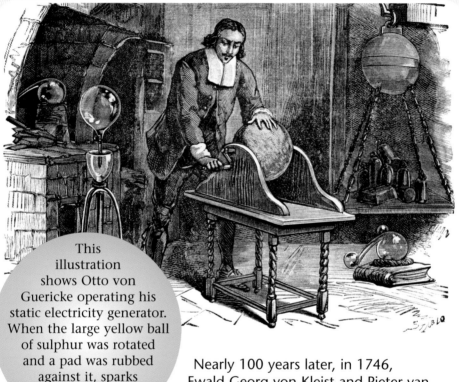

This illustration shows Otto von Guericke operating his static electricity generator. When the large yellow ball of sulphur was rotated and a pad was rubbed against it, sparks were produced.

Nearly 100 years later, in 1746, Ewald Georg von Kleist and Pieter van Musschenbroek invented a device called the Leyden jar. This could store static electricity. It could be very dangerous, though, if a big charge built up in the jar. When Pieter van Musschenbroek touched it with his finger, he received an electric shock that nearly killed him!

In 1786, an English scientist, Abraham Bennett (1749–1799), invented an instrument that he called an electroscope. Using two pieces of gold leaf, this device could detect the size of an electric charge. The design was later improved by Alessandro Volta (1745–1827), an Italian physicist.

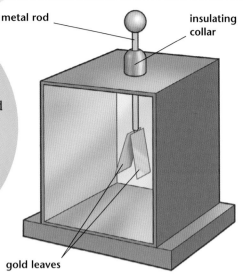

This diagram shows an electroscope. A metal rod passes through an insulating collar and has two thin sheets of gold leaf attached to its end. When the rod is electrically charged, the gold leaves repel each other. If the charge on the leaves is neutralized, the leaves collapse together.

metal rod

insulating collar

gold leaves

In 1786 Luigi Galvani (1737–1798), another Italian scientist, found that if he allowed two metals (iron and copper) to touch the muscles of a dead frog, its legs twitched! He thought electricity must be passing through the muscles.

Building on Galvani's observations, Volta wondered whether electricity would also pass through a liquid. He found that it could. In 1800, Volta developed a device that he called a voltaic pile. This consisted of a pile of alternating zinc and copper discs. Between each disc was a piece of paper soaked in salt solution. Using this device, Volta could produce a steady flow of electricity. Volta went on to develop a voltaic cell, which consisted of strips of zinc and copper in sulphuric acid. This was the first chemical battery. At last, scientists had found a way of producing a steady flow of electricity.

THAT'S AMAZING!

Humphry Davy (1778–1829), an English scientist, was interested in electricity. At a Royal Society demonstration in London, in 1809, he used a voltaic cell to create a brilliant spark nearly 7 centimetres (3 inches) long. This was the first arc light, in which an electrical current produces light as it passes in an arc between two **electrodes**.

Discovering electromagnetism

Volta's chemical cell provided scientists with a constant, steady source of electricity. Electricity that flowed became known as current electricity, in contrast to the static electricity that had been used for the earlier experiments. Using this development, further discoveries soon followed.

A starting point for much of the research was the work of a French scientist called Charles-Augustin Coulomb (1736–1806). During the 1780s, Coulomb had shown that static electricity and magnets had some things in common. He had also realized that there might be a connection between electricity and magnetism.

Hans Christian Oersted (1777–1851), a Dutch scientist, was determined to find this connection. In 1820, he carried out an experiment using a copper wire through which an electric current was flowing. He held a magnetized needle over the wire, and the needle swung round. This proved that electricity and magnetism were somehow connected. Oersted realized that the electric current creates a magnetic field around the wires.

The effect of electricity on a magnet became known as **electromagnetism**. This was the beginning of the science of **electrodynamics**.

WHAT ARE AMPS, COULOMBS, OHMS, AND VOLTS?

The work of Ampère, Coulomb, Ohm, and Volta is remembered in the names of units used today.

- The **ampere (amp)** is a unit of electric current.

- The **coulomb (C)** is a unit of electric charge.

- The **ohm (Ω)** is a unit of electrical resistance.

- The **volt (V)** is a unit of potential difference.

In the same year, a French physicist called André-Marie Ampère (1775–1836) made an interesting discovery. He found that when an electric current is flowing through wires, the wires behave like magnets. They attract or repel each other, depending on whether the current is flowing in the same or the opposite direction. He also found that a wire with a current flowing through it would attract iron, just as a magnet would.

These are some of the instruments that Ampère used to carry out his experiments.

Ampère developed the galvanometer (named after the Italian scientist Luigi Galvani), an instrument that measured the strength of an electric current. Ampère's observations laid the foundations for the laws of electromagnetism. He suggested that magnetism was caused by the movement of extremely small electrical charges. Few people believed him at the time, although scientists today think that his ideas were nearly right.

In 1827, a German physicist called Georg Simon Ohm (1789–1854) discovered that there was a link between the electrical current, the **voltage**, and the **resistance** in a circuit. Resistance is how hard it is for a current to pass through the wire. This eventually became known as Ohm's law.

Electricity, magnetism, and movement

It had been shown that a magnet moved when it was close to an electric current. Scientists began to wonder: could this be useful in some way?

In 1821, an English scientist called Michael Faraday (1791–1867) hung a wire over a strong magnet. When he connected the wire to a battery, he found that the current flowed through the wire.

Michael Faraday was one of Britain's greatest 19th-century scientists. He is most famous for his work on electricity, electromagnetism, electrolysis, and chemistry.

WHO REALLY INVENTED THE DYNAMO?

An American scientist, Joseph Henry (1797–1878), was investigating electromagnetism at the same time as Faraday. Neither Henry nor Faraday knew about each other's work, but they each independently invented a dynamo at almost exactly the same time. It may seem rather unfair to Henry, but Faraday is generally credited with the invention because he published his findings first. Many of their other experiments were also very similar, but Henry was more interested in practical uses, such as making an electric motor and developing a telegraph machine, while Faraday concentrated on theories.

It produced a magnetic field that was opposite to that of the magnet. This made the magnet repel the wire, and the wire moved in circles round the magnet. Faraday called this new device a "rotator". It was interesting, but it was not of much practical use.

Faraday then carried out an experiment using a horseshoe magnet. When he moved a coil of wire through the magnetic field between the two ends of the magnet, an electric current was produced. Using this as a starting point, he developed a machine that would generate electricity. This gave scientists an important tool: a source of electricity that would not run out.

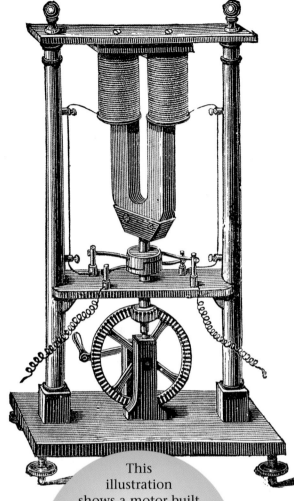

This illustration shows a motor built by Hippolyte Pixii in about 1832. It uses an electromagnet and was based on Faraday's 1831 demonstration that magnetism produces an electric current.

In 1831, Faraday tried passing an electric current through a wire held between two fixed magnets. He thought this might make the wire spin round. It worked – Faraday had succeeded in using electricity to make something move! This was the very first electric motor. It became known as a **dynamo**, or generator. The electrical energy had been changed into **kinetic energy** (moving energy).

Following this success, progress was rapid. As other scientists made improvements to Faraday's basic designs, people began to realize that electricity could be extremely useful.

Linking electricity and other forms of energy

Michael Faraday was a brilliant scientist, but not just because he planned and carried out some very important experiments. He also thought hard about what the results of his experiments might mean, and tried to formulate theories that would explain them.

Since his early experiments, Faraday had been convinced that every type of "force" was linked in some way. If they were all different versions of the same thing, he thought it should be possible to change one into another. What Faraday called "force" we now call energy.

Faraday had done much to establish the idea of magnetic fields. His work with the electric dynamo and electric motor had proved that there was a link between electricity and magnetism. Still convinced that "forces" were linked, Faraday next investigated the effects of an **electromagnet** on light rays. His results suggested that there really was a link between electricity, magnetism, and light. But what could this link be? Faraday continued his research, and in 1850 he suggested that energy was not held in materials themselves but in the spaces between them. He had one major problem, though. He had no way of proving his theories, so other scientists flatly refused to believe him.

This photograph illustrates James Maxwell's electromagnetic field equations.

$$\frac{1}{c}\frac{\partial X}{\partial t} = \frac{\partial \gamma}{\partial y} - \frac{\partial \beta}{\partial z} \; , \quad \frac{1}{c}\frac{\partial Y}{\partial t} = \frac{\partial \alpha}{\partial z} - \frac{\partial \gamma}{\partial x} \; , \quad \frac{1}{c}\frac{\partial Z}{\partial t} = \frac{\partial \beta}{\partial x}$$

$$\frac{1}{c}\frac{\partial \alpha}{\partial t} = \frac{\partial Y}{\partial z} - \frac{\partial Z}{\partial y} \; , \quad \frac{1}{c}\frac{\partial \beta}{\partial t} = \frac{\partial Z}{\partial x} - \frac{\partial X}{\partial z} \; , \quad \frac{1}{c}\frac{\partial \gamma}{\partial t} = \frac{\partial X}{\partial y}$$

A Scottish scientist, James Maxwell (1831–1879), eventually proved that Faraday was right. Many people regard Maxwell as one of the most brilliant scientists and mathematicians of the 19th century.

Maxwell was interested in electricity and magnetism. He took the ideas of earlier scientists and linked them in a set of mathematical equations that explained everything they had observed. These were first presented to the Royal Society in London in 1864.

Maxwell's equations predicted that waves of electric and magnetic fields travel through empty space at a speed that he calculated to be 310,740,000 metres (1,019,200 feet) per second. Amazingly, that was almost the same as the speed of light, which is 299,792,458 metres (983,571,056 feet) per second. The fact that electricity, magnetism, and light travelled at the same speed meant they must all be different versions of the same thing. Maxwell had finally found mathematical proof of the link for which Faraday had searched so hard.

This portrait of the Scottish scientist James Maxwell is by an unknown artist.

TALKING SCIENCE

"All the mathematical sciences are founded on relations between physical laws and laws of numbers, so that the aim of exact science is to reduce the problems of nature to the determination of quantities by operations with numbers."
James Maxwell, in a paper entitled "On Faraday's Lines of Force" (published in 1856)

Linking ideas about energy

While some 19th-century scientists were busy investigating electricity and magnetism, others were just as busy investigating different subjects. Amongst other things, scientists were interested in finding out more about the nature of heat and motion.

In the early 17th century, an English scientist called Francis Bacon (1561–1626) was the first person to suggest that heat and motion might be linked. Later scientists, including René Descartes (1596–1650) in France and Robert Hooke (1635–1703) in England, suggested that heat was the result of particles constantly moving.

In 1783, Antoine Lavoisier (1743–1794), a French scientist, proposed a new theory. He thought that changes in temperature occurred because of the movement of a fluid that he called "caloric".

In 1798, an American scientist, Count Rumford (1753–1814), showed that the caloric theory could not be correct. He suggested instead that heat was really a type of motion. However, many people continued to believe in the caloric theory until well into the 19th century. Experiments carried out in the 1840s by the German physicist Julius Mayer and the English scientist James Joule (1818–1889) showed that Rumford was right. Heat and motion were versions of the same thing.

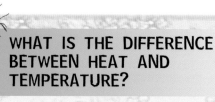

WHAT IS THE DIFFERENCE BETWEEN HEAT AND TEMPERATURE?

It is easy to confuse heat and temperature, but they are really two very different things.

- Heat is a form of energy. It is measured in **joules (J)** in honour of James Prescott Joule.

- Temperature is a measure of how hot or cold something is. It is measured in degrees, usually on a scale known as the **Celsius scale** (°C), or in degrees Fahrenheit (°F).

A German scientist, Hermann von Helmholtz (1821–1894), developed the work of Mayer and Joule. He suggested that there was a link between motion, heat, light, electricity, and magnetism, and proposed the theory of the conservation of energy. According to this theory, energy cannot be created or destroyed; it can only be turned into other types of energy. This later became known as the **first law of thermodynamics**.

According to this law, however much energy goes into something, the same amount of energy must go out of it. For example, when electrical energy goes into an electric lamp, the lamp will give out light energy and heat energy. The amount of electrical energy going into the lamp will be exactly the same as the amount of energy going out as heat and light. The electrical energy has not been lost; it has just changed into other forms of energy.

James Joule found out a great deal about heat and electricity by passing electrical currents through wires.

Understanding steam engines

During the 19th century, many theories were suggested about heat and motion. Some of these theories seemed to fit together, while some directly contradicted each other. Scientists struggled to make sense of it all.

In the early 1820s, a French scientist and engineer called Nicolas Léonard Sadi Carnot (1796–1832) conducted some experiments to find out exactly what happens inside a steam engine. Many people had tried, without much success, to make steam engines more efficient. The early models used a lot of fuel to do just a small amount of work. Carnot was sure this problem could be solved.

Carnot set out to answer two questions:
1. Is there a limit to the amount of useful work that can be obtained from a heat source?
2. Could an engine be made more efficient by using another fluid or gas instead of steam?

Nicolas Léonard Sadi Carnot, the French physicist, is often called the founder of thermodynamics (the study of heat and motion).

His approach was unusual in that he did not just think about real steam engines. He also imagined an ideal engine, based on a theoretical model. By making changes to this model, Carnot could work out mathematically the answers to his two questions. This is the way many scientists work today, using computer modelling techniques to predict different outcomes. But Carnot did not have a computer to help him!

Carnot believed that heat was a fluid called "caloric". Although this was later disproved, it did not affect Carnot's conclusions. He showed that a steam engine's efficiency depends on the temperatures of the two vessels containing hot water. Getting rid of friction and preventing heat transfer between different parts of the engine would also make it more efficient. Using a different liquid or gas would not make any difference. Carnot's research proved that there is indeed a limit on how efficient a heat engine can be.

At the time, Carnot's work was largely ignored by other engineers. However, it was later used by two scientists, called Rudolf Clausius (1822–1888) and William Thomson Kelvin (1824–1907), when they developed the **second law of thermodynamics** (see page 28).

WHY DO GASES EXPAND?

Steam engines work because heating liquid water to create steam increases the **pressure** inside the engine. Scientists in the 19th century did not understand why steam has this effect.

We now know that gases are made up of tiny particles that are free to move to fill whatever space is available. The hotter the gas, the faster the particles move, and the more frequently they collide with each other and their container. This means that, in an enclosed space, the hotter the gas, the greater the pressure it exerts.

This experiment shows what happens when air is heated. A balloon is held in a beaker of water, which is heated. As the temperature rises, the volume of air in the balloon increases, and the balloon expands.

Gases, energy, and thermodynamics

Along with Mayer, Joule, and Helmholtz, other scientists also tried to find out more about the nature of gases. During the 18th century, several scientists had put forward ideas to explain the behaviour of gases. Daniel Bernoulli (1700–1782), working in Holland, first proposed a kinetic theory of gases, which suggested that gas particles were constantly moving. This was further developed by other scientists, including James Joule.

Based on this work, and that of Carnot, Rudolf Clausius, a German physicist, suggested the second law of thermodynamics. He first came up with the idea in 1850, but stated it more formally in 1865. This law can be written in several different ways. One of these is that heat energy will move from a hot place to a cooler place, but not the other way round.

WHAT IS THE KELVIN SCALE?

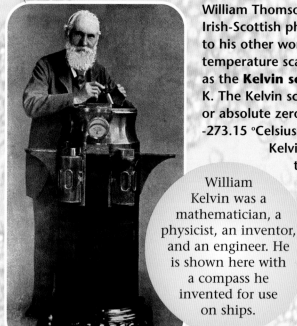

William Thomson Kelvin was an Irish-Scottish physicist. In addition to his other work, he developed a temperature scale that is now known as the **Kelvin scale**. It has the symbol K. The Kelvin scale begins at 0 Kelvin, or absolute zero, which is equivalent to -273.15 °Celsius (-459.67 °Fahrenheit). Kelvin proved that this is the lowest possible temperature that any substance can reach. This is because at absolute zero, a substance has no heat energy and therefore it cannot get any colder than it already is.

William Kelvin was a mathematician, a physicist, an inventor, and an engineer. He is shown here with a compass he invented for use on ships.

For example, if you have a hot cup of coffee, the heat energy from the coffee will move into the air around it. The coffee will therefore get colder and the air will get warmer. This may seem very obvious to us now, but it was the first time that anybody had attempted to explain exactly what was happening to the heat energy and why.

If the second law of thermodynamics was true, and heat energy moved, it meant that the particles in a gas had to be moving. During the 1860s, James Maxwell and an Austrian physicist called Ludwig Boltzmann (1844–1906) independently worked out a theory which became known as the Maxwell-Boltzmann kinetic theory of gases. This theory explained the way gases behaved in scientific experiments in terms of the size and speed of the gas particles. It showed that there was a connection between the temperature of the gas and the speed at which the gas particles moved. The Maxwell-Boltzmann kinetic theory finally provided mathematical proof that heat and motion were linked.

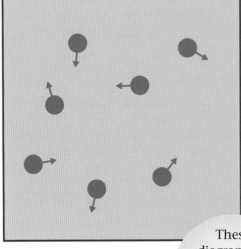

cool gas, little energy, little movement, low pressure

These diagrams of gas particles illustrate the kinetic theory of gases.

James Maxwell combined these ideas with the work of Ampère and Faraday (see pages 19–21). He had already proved that magnetism, electricity, and light were connected. Now, according to his mathematics, there could also be a connection between these and heat – and therefore also, based on the Maxwell-Boltzmann theory, with motion.

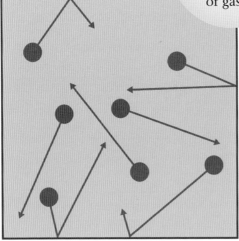

hot gas, more energy, more movement, high pressure

Radios and telephones

While scientists such as Maxwell and Kelvin were investigating thermodynamics, other scientists were investigating the practical uses of energy. From this work came some amazing breakthroughs in communication systems.

During the 19th century, an electric telegraph system had been developed. Although messages could be sent and received as coded electrical signals, the sender and the receiver were only connected by a wire. They could not actually hear or talk to each other. From the electric telegraph network came the telephone . . . and eventually the radio.

In 1876, Alexander Graham Bell (1847–1922), a Scot working in Massachusetts, in the United States, was the first person to **patent** a workable design for a telephone. It used a **diaphragm** connected to a wire that formed part of an electrical circuit. If a sound was made, the diaphragm vibrated. This made the wire move, and changed the electrical current in the circuit. This change could be sent along wires to a receiver.

Here, the electrical changes would be turned back into movement. This would make another diaphragm vibrate and reproduce the sound. The telephone really was an amazing step forward: it could carry the human voice!

Another extraordinary discovery was made just a few years later. Maxwell's equations had predicted that **electromagnetic** waves, including light, could be produced by varying an electric current.

HOW WAS THE FIRST TELEPHONE CALL MADE?

The first telephone call was made on 10 March 1876. Alexander Graham Bell sat in one room while his assistant, Thomas Watson, was in the room next door. Bell's first words, using his new telephone, were "Mr. Watson, come here, I want you!"

Maxwell had also predicted that these waves would travel through the air. In 1888, a German physicist called Heinrich Hertz (1857–1894) carried out a demonstration. He showed that when a spark was produced by an electrical circuit, another spark was released a fraction of a second later by a separate circuit a few feet away. There was no connection between the circuits, so the second spark must have been caused by waves travelling though the air. This was the first demonstration that such waves existed. At first they were known as "Hertzian waves", but later they became known as radio waves.

Other scientists began investigating these waves. Between 1895 and 1896, Alexander Popov (1859–1905), a Russian, and Guglielmo Marconi (1874–1937), an Italian, independently developed a method of sending and receiving the waves over longer distances. Marconi pursued the discovery more actively than Popov, and travelled to England to patent his idea. The invention became known as a "wireless", because sounds were transmitted and received without being connected by wires. From Marconi's first simple device, more sophisticated equipment was soon developed. In 1901, the first transatlantic radio transmission was sent. The radio age had begun.

Marconi is shown here with some of his wireless apparatus.

Electricity from steam

Michael Faraday had invented the dynamo in 1831 (see page 21) as a method of generating electricity. People soon began to see all sorts of ways in which electricity could be used. Now they had to find new ways of producing it on a large scale.

Scientists rapidly developed Faraday's original dynamo, creating bigger and more powerful machines. By the 1850s, steam-powered generators were in use. These used coal to power a steam engine. The engine turned a dynamo, which produced electricity. Although the early dynamos were inefficient, an American inventor, Thomas Edison (1847–1931), developed a more efficient design.

At the same time as electricity generation was expanding, another inventor was trying to develop a form of electric lighting that could be used in the home.

Thomas Edison stands by his dynamo in the Edison Works plant in New Jersey, in the United States, in about 1906.

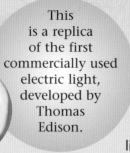

This is a replica of the first commercially used electric light, developed by Thomas Edison.

The arc light, invented by Humphry Davy (see page 17), was too bright for domestic use. An English inventor, Joseph Swan (1828–1914), spent more than 30 years working on the problem of producing a smaller, reliable light for the home. His design was first demonstrated between 1878 and 1880. It had a **filament** (a tiny coil of metal wire) inside a glass ball that contained no air. When it was connected to an electricity supply, the current flowed through the filament and glowed. It was an instant success, and our light bulbs today still follow the same basic design. Thomas Edison improved Swan's design by replacing the metal filament with longer-lasting carbonized cotton thread.

Soon, businessmen were setting up companies to generate electricity, for industry and homes. Although these companies were small, they were the beginnings of the electricity supply industry.

THAT'S AMAZING!

Edison was a brilliant inventor, **patenting** more than 1,000 inventions. In addition to the electric light bulb, these included:

- telegraphy apparatus
- the electrical vote recorder
- the phonograph (to record sounds)
- the kinetoscope (to record moving pictures)
- the kinetophone (to link sound and moving pictures to create the first talking movies)
- the microtasimeter (to detect very small temperature changes)
- the wireless telegraph (to communicate with moving trains)
- the mimeograph (to copy written documents).

When asked how he managed to do all this, Edison replied, "Genius is 1 per cent inspiration and 99 per cent perspiration!" In other words, hard work was more important than bright ideas.

The "AC or DC?" argument

The first electricity-generating companies supplied direct current (DC) electricity. This is a continuous, one-way flow of electric current. This was suitable for the original purpose of small, local supplies. But could it be used on a larger scale?

As the demand for electricity grew, people began to look again at the DC generators and their method of producing electricity. The direct low-**voltage**, high-current electricity that DC generators supplied was not very suitable for supplying power over long distances. This was because high-current electricity loses a lot more power on the way than low-current electricity, and DC could not easily be switched to high-voltage, low-current electricity.

This New York sitting room was photographed in 1905. The fittings include an electric radiator, an electric iron and desk lights, and an electric sewing machine motor.

A scientist from Eastern Europe, Nikola Tesla (1856–1943), came up with a solution. He pioneered a method of reversing the current flow backwards and forwards very quickly. The direction of the current alternates, so the technology was called alternating current (AC).

In the United States, Edison's electricity company stuck with DC. He was convinced that this was safer and better than AC. However, one of Edison's main rivals, George Westinghouse (1846–1914), thought that AC would be better in the long term. Westinghouse built a power station to generate AC electricity. Edison used every means he could think of to persuade people to agree with him. The arguments continued, and for a few years both systems were in use at the same time.

However, AC gradually came to dominate the electricity supply industry because AC electricity could be distributed efficiently over much greater distances than DC electricity. As many machines and appliances need high voltage to work, this switch was essential. The first AC power station in England was opened in Deptford, London, in 1890. Today, the AC system is used worldwide.

TIMELINE

As electricity became more widely available, the designs of many appliances were changed so that they could be driven by this new source of power. This meant that ordinary jobs could be done more easily and more quickly. This timeline shows when an electrical version of some everyday appliances first appeared.

1882	clothes iron
1889	oven
1895	hand drill
1904	razor
1907	washing machine
1908	vacuum cleaner
1922	kettle
1925	screwdriver
1926	lawnmower

Steamships and power stations

There was a growing demand for electricity, but the steam-powered generators were not very efficient. In the early 1880s, there seemed to be no way of increasing their efficiency. Then an Irish engineer, called Charles Algernon Parsons (1854–1932), came up with a new idea – the steam turbine.

There had been several attempts to adapt the design of generators to make them faster and bigger. However, these all brought new difficulties, such as excessive noise or movement. Pumping lubricating oil into the engines helped but did not completely solve the problems.

Charles Parsons was sure there had to be a better way. In 1884, he made a fundamental change to the work done by the steam engine. Instead of using it to push **pistons**, he made it turn a **rotor** round and round. This was the first steam turbine. Piston engines could only turn a dynamo at 500 revolutions per minute (rpm), whereas Parsons's turbine could turn it at 18,000 rpm! Although the new turbine needed enormous quantities of steam, it was much more efficient than the old piston engines.

In 1888, Parsons installed four of his steam turbines in the Forth Banks power station in Newcastle upon Tyne, England. This was the first power station to be driven by turbines instead of piston engines. By the early 1900s, steam turbines dominated the electricity generating industry.

THAT'S AMAZING!

Charles Algernon Parsons thought his new steam turbines would be ideal for powering ships. He used his designs in a new ship, the *Turbinia*, which could reach much higher speeds than any other ship at that time. He approached the Royal Navy with his designs, but they ignored him. Parsons was determined to prove that he was right. In 1897, at a naval display in Spithead that was attended by Queen Victoria, a smaller boat suddenly appeared among the navy vessels. It was the *Turbinia* – and when Royal Navy boats tried to chase it, they could not catch it! The Royal Navy finally realized that Parsons's ideas did work, and commissioned him to build steam turbines for its fleet.

This is the world's first turbine-powered boat, the *Turbinia*. In 1897, at Spithead, the *Turbinia* achieved the unheard-of speed of 63.5 kilometres (39 miles) per hour (34.5 knots). After this, orders for turbine-powered ships followed quickly for both military and civilian use.

Energy science

As we have seen (on page 23), James Maxwell had shown the link between electricity, magnetism, light, heat, and motion. They were all believed to be types of ray. The rays were thought to behave like waves, each type having a different wavelength (the distance between the peaks). Maxwell's equations also predicted the existence of other rays, some with longer wavelengths than visible light, and some with shorter wavelengths.

All the known rays could be arranged in order of the length of their waves. This became known as the **"electromagnetic spectrum"**, as the rays were organized in the same way as the different lengths of the light rays that make up a spectrum.

The discovery of very short rays was made possible by the invention of a mercury pump in 1855 by a German technician called Heinrich Geissler (1815–1879). Using this pump, good-quality **vacuum** tubes, which were useful for studying various rays, could be made.

This diagram shows the electromagnetic spectrum.

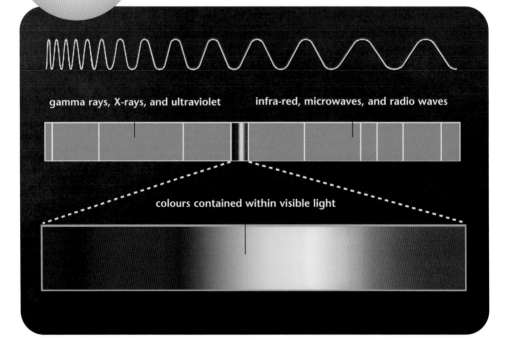

gamma rays, X-rays, and ultraviolet   infra-red, microwaves, and radio waves

colours contained within visible light

William Crookes (1832–1919), an English physicist, improved the vacuum tubes still further and they became known as "Crookes tubes".

Geissler was an assistant to a German physicist, Julius Plücker (1801–1868). In 1858, Plücker discovered that, if he sealed two **electrodes** inside a vacuum tube and forced an electric current between them, the tube glowed green! Plücker thought this effect must be caused by rays that were given off by the **cathode** (the negative electrode). Plücker called the rays "cathode rays".

William Crookes found that using different metals for the electrodes did not affect the rays. He thought they must therefore be a result of the electric current, rather than the cathode ray tube. In 1879, he found that the rays could be bent by a magnetic field. The way in which they were bent indicated that they had a negative charge. Crookes thought that the rays must be made up of a stream of separate, charged particles.

Other scientists were not so sure. Soon, there were two separate theories.

1. Particle theory: cathode rays were electrically charged particles.
   Evidence: the rays could be bent by magnets.

2. **Wave theory**: cathode rays were waves.
   Evidence: the rays travelled in straight lines and gravity did not affect them.

Most French and English physicists believed the particle theory, while most German physicists believed the wave theory.

An English physicist, Joseph John ("J.J.") Thomson (1856–1940), found an answer in 1897. He measured how much the rays were bent by electricity and by magnetism. His experiments showed that the rays were made up of particles, each with a negative charge. Thomson called the particles **electrons**. His work also suggested that atoms were made up of even smaller particles. Thomson was awarded a Nobel Prize in 1906 for his discovery of electrons. However, scientists later found that he was only partly right (see page 42).

Discovering radioactivity

At the same time as J.J. Thomson was measuring rays, other scientists were experimenting with cathode ray tubes – and making some amazing discoveries of their own.

In 1895, a German physicist called William Röntgen (1845–1923) noticed that, even when his cathode ray tube was shielded with black paper, a nearby fluorescent material glowed. He thought this was strange, and tried putting other materials between the cathode ray tube and the fluorescent material. Some materials reduced the glow, but nothing got rid of it completely. Röntgen thought invisible rays of some sort must be reaching the fluorescent material. But what could these rays be? And how could they pass through things so easily?

The rays were officially called "Röntgen rays", but they were commonly known as X-rays because "x" is the mathematical symbol for "an unknown quantity". These were one type of the very short rays that Maxwell's equations had predicted.

WHEN WAS THE FIRST X-RAY TAKEN?

The first X-ray image of part of the human body was taken by William Röntgen in 1895. He positioned his wife's hand between a cathode ray tube and a photographic plate. When the electric current was turned on, the stream of rays passed through her hand and formed an image on the photographic plate. The image clearly showed the bones of her hand – and it even showed her gold wedding ring! The discovery that X-rays could pass through soft tissue but not through bone was a major advance for doctors. Many doctors soon started to use X-ray images as a tool in medical diagnosis.

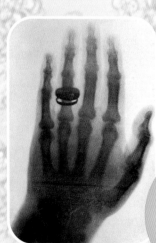

This is one of the early X-ray images taken by William Röntgen.

Marie Curie was born in Poland and emigrated to France in 1891. She is shown here in her laboratory in Paris. She shared a Nobel Prize in Physics in 1903 with her husband Pierre for their research on radioactivity.

A French scientist, Antoine-Henri Becquerel (1852–1908), thought the glow Röntgen had noticed might be coming from the fluorescent material itself. When he left a photographic plate close to a uranium compound, the plate became foggy. This suggested that the uranium compound was giving off some sort of ray. Becquerel showed that this was not the same as Röntgen's X-rays. He had discovered another type of short ray.

Other scientists, including Marie Curie (1867–1934) in France, began working on this new type of "radiation". It was soon found that uranium compounds produced three types of ray, which were called alpha, beta, and gamma.

Becquerel proved that the beta rays were exactly the same as the rays from a cathode ray tube: they were streams of electrons. In 1900, a New Zealand physicist, called Ernest Rutherford (1871–1937), showed that the gamma rays were like X-rays but were even shorter.

Quantum theory and atoms

At the end of the 19th century, scientists gradually began to find that many of the recent scientific developments, such as X-rays and the structure of atoms, were actually linked. While some scientists were investigating electricity, waves, and electrons, others were still interested in heat. They thought that a ray of heat could be given off and absorbed in any amount. This meant that it could be divided into smaller units, which could be divided into smaller units, which could be divided into even smaller units, and so on, with no limit.

Scientists studying the electromagnetic spectrum (see page 38) found that temperature was important. For example, when a metal is heated it changes from red to orange to yellow and eventually to white. As the temperature increases, the wavelength decreases. However, there seemed to be exceptions to this rule.

WHAT IS THE INSIDE OF AN ATOM LIKE?

In 1898, J.J. Thomson suggested that the inside of an atom was a positively charged ball with negatively charged electrons stuck in it, like raisins in a pudding. This was disproved in 1903, when Philipp Lenard (1862–1947) discovered that atoms actually contain a lot of empty space. A Japanese physicist, Hantaro Nagaoka, suggested that an atom had a positively charged centre, with electrons travelling in rings around it. In 1911, Ernest Rutherford, a New Zealander working in England, modified Nagaoka's model slightly. According to Rutherford, the inside of an atom resembled our Solar System, with electrons orbiting the central **nucleus** like planets orbiting the Sun (see page 47). This has become a familiar idea, although physicists now know that they have no real similarities except for a concentration of mass at the core.

The work of two scientists, Albert Einstein (1879–1955) and Max Planck (1858–1947), suggested an explanation that did fit all the results. Suppose heat was not infinitely divisible? Einstein and Planck suggested that energy in the rays could only be given off in exact amounts. The rays were more like a stream of tiny, separate parcels than a continuous wave. They called the smallest indivisible unit a "quantum". This idea became known as the **quantum theory** and formed the basis of the branch of physics known as **quantum mechanics**.

Max Planck, who was a professor at the University of Berlin, Germany, is often called the founding father of quantum physics.

At first, other scientists did not take much notice of Einstein's and Planck's revolutionary idea. However, in 1905 Albert Einstein showed that the quantum theory could be used to explain other experimental findings. This persuaded others to take the quantum theory seriously, and it gradually became accepted.

In 1911, Niels Bohr (1885–1962), a Danish physicist, used the quantum theory to explain the structure and behaviour of atoms. His explanations were not perfect, but they sparked off interest in the subject, and other scientists developed the idea further.

This is a computer illustration of a spaceship travelling at or near the speed of light. Under these conditions, time passes slightly slower.

Linking energy and mass

Following the development of the quantum theory, Albert Einstein continued his theoretical investigations of physics, and came up with some revolutionary ideas. He published two articles stating his **Special Theory of Relativity** in 1905. This extended the law of the conservation of energy.

The first of Einstein's papers on relativity was partly about the speed of light. Einstein proposed that:

● the speed of light never changes – whatever happens, this is constant

● in certain conditions, time may pass at different rates

● the absolute speed of something moving cannot be measured – you can only measure speed relative to the speed of something else.

The last of these statements can be puzzling, but try thinking of it in this way. If you sit on a moving train, you are not moving relative to the train. However, you are moving relative to the countryside that the train passes through. If you talk about your speed, you must therefore say whether you mean relative to the train or to the countryside.

The second of Einstein's papers on relativity linked energy and mass. It was a simple equation but it contained an earth-shattering idea: $E = mc^2$.

This equation meant that the amount of energy something contains (E) equals its mass (m) multiplied by the speed of light squared (c^2). Even a very small object would therefore contain a huge amount of energy! It also meant that the **first law of thermodynamics** (the law of the conservation of energy) had to be rewritten as the law of the conservation of mass and energy. In this form, it now stated that the sum of all the mass and energy in the Universe is constant, and that transformations between mass and energy are governed by the equation $E = mc^2$.

Other scientists found Einstein's ideas very hard to believe at first. They seemed to go against common sense. However, the experimental evidence proved that he was right, and eventually his ideas were accepted.

ALBERT EINSTEIN'S STORY

Like many great thinkers, Albert Einstein was a very private person. He enjoyed sailing and playing the violin, and he was involved in charities and politics. Einstein was also a rather strange man, who found it hard to fit in with ordinary social expectations. For example, he kept very few clothes so that he would not have to waste time deciding what to wear. He also stopped wearing socks because he got fed up with his toes making holes in them!

Einstein, one of the world's greatest scientists, was born in Germany, studied in Switzerland, and became a US citizen in 1940.

Energy from atoms

These diagrams show Rutherford's model of the electron orbiting the nucleus (top), and the more complex model of the atom proposed by James Chadwick, Niels Bohr, and Ernest Rutherford (bottom).

The discovery of the **electron** in 1897 (see page 39) made scientists realize that atoms consisted of even smaller particles. But what were these particles? And how did they behave? In the early years of the 20th century, physicists were urgently searching for answers to these questions.

The Rutherford model of the atom explained much, but not all, of the experimental evidence. Electrons seemed to be particles, but they also seemed to behave like waves. Which were they?

Several scientists, including Louis de Broglie (1892–1987) and Werner Heisenberg (1901–1976), carried out important work in this field. Eventually, in 1926, Erwin Schrödinger (1887–1961), working in Austria, developed an equation that allowed electrons to behave both as particles and as waves. This was called the Schrödinger equation, and it was based on **wave theory**.

At the same time, Heisenberg developed a similar theory, which Schrödinger later said proved exactly the same as the wave theory. These theories were the basis for a branch of physics that became known as **wave mechanics**.

While some physicists were busy debating particles and waves, others were discovering more about the structure of atoms. A positively charged particle had been discovered. This was given the name **proton** by Ernest Rutherford. In 1932, James Chadwick (1891–1974), an English physicist, discovered another sub-atomic particle, the **neutron**. Atoms now seemed to contain three types of particles: electrons, protons, and neutrons. Protons and neutrons formed the centre of the atom, called the **nucleus**. Electrons travelled around this in circles, like planets orbiting the Sun.

THAT'S AMAZING!

Schrödinger used an example known as "Schrödinger's cat" to explain his wave theory. Imagine a sealed box containing a live cat, a radioactive source, a **Geiger counter**, a hammer, and a bottle full of poisonous fumes. If radioactive decay occurs, the Geiger counter will detect it, trigger a device that moves the hammer and smashes the jar, and the poisonous fumes will kill the cat. The chances of this happening or not happening are equal. Normally, we would say there is a 50:50 chance of the cat being alive or dead. In **quantum theory**, from the point when the lid is closed until it is next opened and the live or dead cat is revealed, you have to imagine that the cat is both alive and dead at the same time. Two opposite things can both be true!

According to quantum physics, things that are impossible to predict, like radioactive decay, are affected by being observed. Until the box is opened, the fate of Schrödinger's cat is therefore not just unknown; it is undecided.

Nuclear power

Once scientists knew about the existence of electrons, protons, and neutrons, research moved forward quickly. The energy locked within an atom would soon be unleashed…

Several scientists, including the Italian-born American nuclear physicist Enrico Fermi (1901–1954), began to study the properties of these sub-atomic particles. They also wanted to find out how the particles interacted with each other. When they bombarded heavy **elements**, such as uranium, with neutrons, they found that the nuclei of the element's atoms would split into two. This process is called **nuclear fission**. Each nucleus that split gave off free neutrons, as well as a huge amount of energy.

Enrico Fermi won a Nobel Prize in 1938. He is shown here in his laboratory in Chicago, in the United States, in 1942.

In 1942, Fermi and his team of researchers in the United States found that, as the nuclei split, some of the free neutrons then hit other nuclei. Those nuclei would in turn split into two, and release more free neutrons and more energy. Those free neutrons would hit more nuclei, and so on. This is called a "chain reaction". Fermi found that he could control the chain reaction by inserting metal rods into the uranium. The metal rods capture free neutrons, and this slows down the reaction.

Once they had understood the principle of the chain reaction, scientists realized that they could potentially release vast amounts of energy. This had some dramatic implications for weapons research and the energy industry.

Fermi's method of controlling the reaction with metal rods meant that this energy release did not have to be destructive, as in an atom bomb. Instead, it could be used to generate electricity. It could provide an alternative to burning fossil fuels such as coal, oil, and gas.

The world's first nuclear power station opened on 17 October 1956 at Calder Hall, Windscale, in England. It was soon followed by more nuclear power stations in other countries.

? HOW CAN ATOMS DESTROY A CITY?

The awesome power contained within atoms became apparent to the world on 6 August 1945 when the United States dropped an atomic bomb on to the Japanese city of Hiroshima. The bomb was made from two masses of uranium-235 forced together by a chemical explosion. This began an uncontrollable chain reaction, resulting in an explosion equivalent to thousands of tonnes of conventional explosives. Around 75,000 people were killed instantly. Three days later, another atomic bomb was dropped on the city of Nagasaki, killing 38,000 people. Many more people died later on, from radiation-related illnesses. These actions ended the Second World War, but they caused devastation on an unimaginable scale.

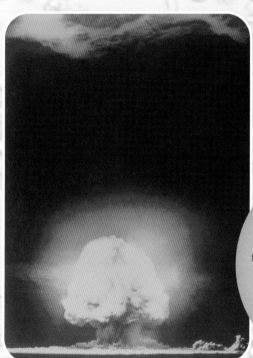

This photograph shows the world's first atomic bomb being detonated at Los Alamos, in the United States. The details of this explosion were kept secret until after the destruction of Hiroshima on 6 August 1945.

WHAT SHOULD BE DONE WITH RADIOACTIVE WASTE?

Many people argue that, unlike burning fossil fuels, nuclear power is a clean and environmentally friendly way of generating electricity. It releases no smoke or harmful gases into the atmosphere. However, nuclear fission does produce radioactive waste. In some cases, this waste may remain radioactive for thousands of years. Reprocessing may reduce the level of radioactivity, but the waste is still very dangerous. Disposing of this waste safely poses many problems. We can get rid of it by burying it in thick concrete under ground, or by dumping it deep under the oceans. However, we do not know what the long-term effects of this might be. Opponents of nuclear power say radioactive waste could be a threat to the future of our planet. They believe that nuclear fission reactions should be banned. Scientists are searching for better disposal methods, but at present there is no simple solution to the problem.

Storing nuclear waste presents many technical challenges. This technician at La Hague, in France, is checking that no radiation is leaking from these nuclear waste storage containers. At La Hague, used nuclear fuel is bonded with glass and stored in a facility like this.

How safe is nuclear fission?

Nuclear fission reactions do release massive amounts of energy. However, many people have questioned whether it is sensible to use nuclear fission in our power stations. The possibility of an accident is very frightening, as it could endanger huge numbers of people and pollute vast areas of land.

There have been at least two major incidents and many smaller incidents since the nuclear power industry began. The first was an accident at Three Mile Island in the United States in 1979. Nobody was injured but people were very worried about how dangerous the situation could have become.

The second nuclear accident, in 1986, at Chernobyl in the Ukraine (formerly part of the Soviet Union), was far more serious. Following an explosion in the nuclear reactor, dozens of people were killed and radiation escaped. All land within 30 kilometres (18 miles) was evacuated, and people worried about radioactivity being carried across Europe by clouds and wind.

A different type of nuclear power?

The question remains: is there an alternative to fission? Some scientists think there may be. Instead of splitting atoms, as in nuclear fission, they could be joined together. This is called **nuclear fusion**. The process is essentially the same as that which takes place in the Sun. When two hydrogen nuclei join together, one heavier nucleus is made, and energy is released. There is just one problem – it is very difficult to control nuclear fusion reactions. If researchers could find a way of doing this, we would have a clean energy source that would never run out.

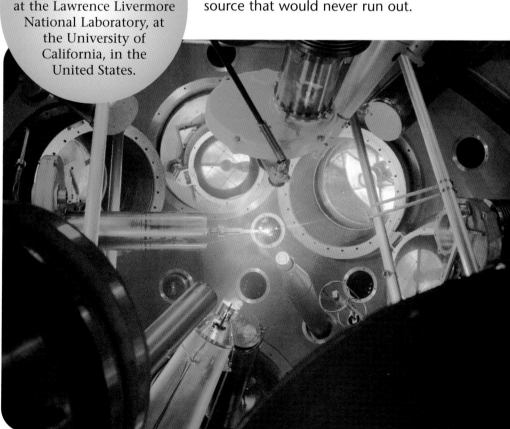

This high-powered laser creates nuclear fusion inside its target chamber at the Lawrence Livermore National Laboratory, at the University of California, in the United States.

New ideas about energy

Electrons, neutrons, and **protons** were just the beginning. Once scientists began investigating atomic structure, they found some very strange things indeed! Research is still continuing. New particles are still being discovered, and new theories are still being suggested to account for them.

Once, an atom was thought to be the smallest unit that existed. Then scientists proved that an atom was made up of a **nucleus** and orbiting electrons. Next, the nucleus turned out to be made up of two types of particles, neutrons and protons. Perhaps we should not be surprised to find that neutrons and protons are made from even smaller particles!

Many teams of scientists have tried to understand the structure of atoms. Rather than just waiting for sub-atomic particles to be detected, scientists decided to build a machine that could produce the particles artificially. This might seem very odd – how can you build a machine to make something when you are not even sure that the thing exists? However, that is exactly what the scientists did.

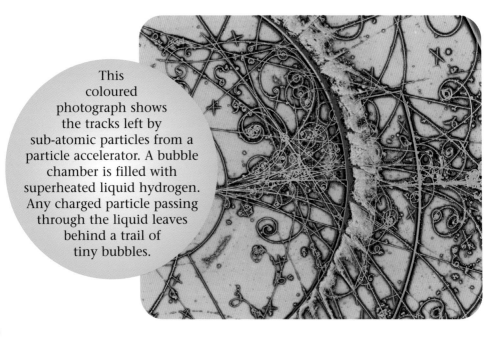

This coloured photograph shows the tracks left by sub-atomic particles from a particle accelerator. A bubble chamber is filled with superheated liquid hydrogen. Any charged particle passing through the liquid leaves behind a trail of tiny bubbles.

Hundreds of different sub-atomic particles have now been discovered. They have some pretty weird names, such as hadrons, bosons, quarks, and leptons! We usually think of our world in the three dimensions of length, breadth, and width. Time is sometimes called the fourth dimension. However, to begin to understand modern theories about the structure of atoms, you would have to think in 11 dimensions! To most people, this is simply unimaginable. Yet some scientists are fascinated by these ideas, and are determined to find out more about them.

This safety supervisor is riding a bicycle along the large hadron collider (LHC) tunnel at CERN, the European particle physics laboratory, near Geneva, in Switzerland.

The machines are called **particle accelerators**. The early ones accelerated the particles down straight tunnels that were several kilometres long. Later, circular accelerators, called **cyclotrons**, were developed. The biggest is at Fermilab, Chicago, in the United States, and it is a 6-kilometre (4-mile) ring. Using these accelerators, particles travel at extremely high speeds. This allows scientists to detect and identify even smaller sub-atomic particles.

Black and white, hot and cold – these are some examples of opposites. Scientists have discovered that sub-atomic particles have opposites too, and these make up what is called **antimatter**. For example, the positron is the opposite of an electron (and is therefore also known as an anti-electron). It was first detected in 1932. Since then, anti-neutrons and anti-protons have also been discovered. Each is exactly the same as the normal particle, but carries the opposite electric charge and magnetic properties. If a particle meets its opposite, they destroy each other and release a lot of energy.

Energy in the 21st century

The science of energy has progressed a lot since the days of windmills and horse ploughs, steam engines, and the first **dynamos**. Where do we stand now, and where might this science take us next?

Some people believe that unlocking the secrets of atoms could provide us with clean, limitless fuel. Achieving **nuclear fusion** would also enable us to lessen our use of fossil fuels. This would in turn help to reduce global warming. Scientists worldwide are therefore actively pursuing these lines of research.

This is a painting of a possible solar sail. A space shuttle is flying in the distant background.

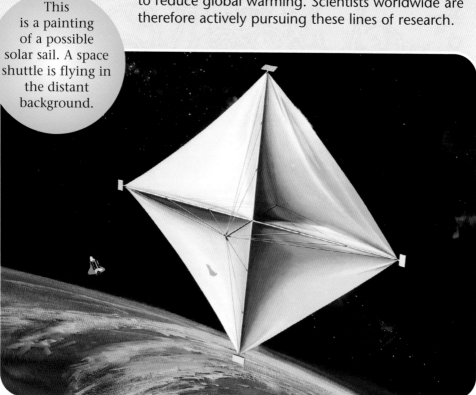

THAT'S AMAZING!

In the future, the Sun's energy could provide a means of transport in space. The slight **pressure** exerted by sunlight is magnified in space because there is no friction. This pressure could be used to push huge, highly reflective solar sails attached to spaceships. The Sun's force is strongest within our Solar System, but would still be strong enough to propel a spaceship to a neighbouring star.

Another strand of modern science involves looking at alternative energy sources. These include fuel cells that convert chemical energy directly into electrical energy. One **electrode** has a supply of fuel such as hydrogen or methane. The other electrode has a supply of oxygen. As long as the supply of fuel and oxygen continues, the fuel cell will continue to produce electricity without running down. Fuel cells are non-polluting, and they are already being used to power vehicles such as some buses and taxis.

Solar cells convert the Sun's energy into electricity. They can be used as power stations, and to provide sources of power in places that have no other supply. They have no moving parts and do not need any fuel, so they can be used in space, for example for powering satellites.

This is an MRI scan of a person's hand.

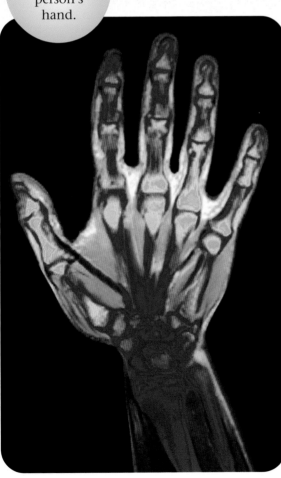

Energy is being used in new ways. From the first X-rays more than a century ago, sophisticated medical diagnostic instruments have been developed. For example, using a strong magnetic field, magnetic resonance imaging (MRI) provides detailed images of soft tissues. It works because the magnetic field alters the arrangement of water **molecules** inside the body. The technique avoids the damaging radiation of X-rays and gamma-rays. Doctors are even trying to develop small, hand-held MRI scanners to replace the large, expensive hospital models currently being used. Energy may be used in other ways, too, in the medicine of the future.

Timeline

before 750,000 BC Fire used as source of heat and light.

before 4000 BC Sailing boats in Mesopotamia used wind energy.

mid-7th century AD First windmill in Persia.

early 13th century First water mill in France.

1698 Thomas Savery patents a workable steam engine.

1752 Benjamin Franklin proves that lightning is a form of electricity.

1775 James Watt and Matthew Boulton develop more efficient steam engines.

1800 Alessandro Volta uses a voltaic pile to produce a steady flow of electricity.

1804 Richard Trevithick builds the first steam locomotive.

1807 Thomas Young first uses the word "energy" with its modern meaning.

1809 Humphry Davy demonstrates an arc light.

1820 Hans Christian Oersted proves that electricity and magnetism are connected.

1820 André-Marie Ampère shows that an electric current can make wires behave as magnets.

1820s Nicolas Léonard Sadi Carnot proves there is a limit to the efficiency of a steam engine.

1827 Georg Simon Ohm discovers the link between voltage and resistance.

1831 Michael Faraday and Joseph Henry independently invent the dynamo.

1855 Julius Plücker discovers cathode rays.

1865 The second law of thermodynamics is proposed.

1860s Maxwell-Boltzmann theory of gases is proposed.

1876 Alexander Graham Bell patents the first telephone system.

1878—1880 Joseph Swan demonstrates the domestic light bulb.

1888 Heinrich Hertz discovers radio waves.

1895 William Röntgen discovers X-rays.

1895—1896 Guglielmo Marconi patents the first "wireless".

1898 J.J. Thomson discovers electrons.

1901 The first transatlantic radio transmission takes place.

1900s Max Planck and Albert Einstein develop quantum theory.

1905 Einstein proposes his Special Theory of Relativity.

1919 Ernest Rutherford discovers protons.

1926 Erwin Schrödinger's equation begins the science of wave mechanics.

1932 James Chadwick discovers neutrons.

1942 First nuclear chain reaction takes place.

1945 United States drops an atomic bomb on Hiroshima, Japan.

1952 CERN established in Geneva, Switzerland.

1956 First nuclear power station opens at Calder Hall, Windscale, in the United Kingdom.

1967 National Accelerator Laboratory founded. Renamed Fermilab, in honour of Enrico Fermi, in 1974.

1977 First MRI scan of human body carried out.

1979 Accident at Three Mile Island nuclear power station, in the United States.

1986 Major accident at Chernobyl nuclear station, in Russia.

1995 Top quark discovered at Fermilab.

2006 Prototype fuel-cell powered cars launched.

2006 First solar sail spacecraft launched.

2006 Formal plans adopted for construction of nuclear fusion plant in France.

Biographies

These are some of the leading scientists in the story of energy.

Thomas Edison (1847–1931)

Thomas Edison was born in Milan, Ohio, in the United States. Because he kept asking questions at school, his teachers thought he was stupid, and so his mother decided to teach him herself at home. Thomas began work at the age of 13, as a newsboy on the railway. He later worked as a telegraph operator for several different companies, but read science books and worked on his own inventions in his spare time. In 1871, Edison married Mary G. Stillwell and they had three children. In 1877, Edison became famous for his invention of the phonograph. After his first wife's death in 1884, Edison married Mina Milner in 1886, and they had three more children. As his success grew, Edison set up the Menlo Park research laboratory and rapidly produced many more inventions. By the time he died at the age of 84, Edison had patented more than 1,093 inventions, nearly half of which were connected with light and power.

Albert Einstein (1879–1955)

Albert Einstein was born in Ulm, in southern Germany. His family were Jewish. Albert was educated in Munich, Germany, and in Aarau, Switzerland. In 1896, he began to train as a teacher but could not find a teaching job. Instead, he worked at the Swiss Patent Office. He married Mileva Maric in 1903 and they had three children. He carried out his scientific research in his spare time, and in 1911 he was given the post of Professor Extraordinary at Zurich University. He worked at universities in Prague and Berlin and in 1914 became a German citizen. He divorced his wife in 1919 and married his cousin, Elsa Lowenthal. In 1933, with the rise of Hitler and the Nazis in Germany, Einstein emigrated to the United States where he worked at Princeton University. He became a US citizen in 1940. Einstein's brilliant theories of relativity and quantum physics have formed the basis of much of modern physics. Einstein died in 1955 in New Jersey, in the United States.

Michael Faraday (1791–1867)

Michael Faraday was born in Surrey, England. His father was a blacksmith and Michael received only a basic education. When he was 12, Michael was apprenticed to a bookbinder, where he spent much of his time reading the books that were being bound. He persuaded the famous chemist, Humphry Davy, to employ him as an assistant and he worked for Davy for many years. As well as many other scientific achievements, Faraday invented the dynamo and the electric motor. He also suggested that light, electricity, and magnetism were linked. Towards the end of his life, Faraday became ill, possibly from mercury poisoning as a result of his research. He died in 1867 in London.

Enrico Fermi (1901–1954)

Enrico Fermi was born in Rome, Italy. His father worked on the railways and his mother was a teacher. There were three older children in the family. Enrico went to school locally and in 1918 went to study physics at Pisa University. He was awarded his doctorate in 1922, and continued his studies in Germany and the Netherlands. In 1928, Fermi married Laura Capon and they had two children. Fermi carried out research into radioactivity and was awarded the Nobel Prize for Physics in 1938. At the beginning of the Second World War, Enrico and his family moved to the United States, where he worked at Columbia University. Fermi developed a method for starting a controlled nuclear chain reaction. This formed the basis of the modern nuclear power industry. Fermi died of cancer in 1954.

William Thomson Kelvin (1824–1907)

William Thomson Kelvin was born in Belfast, Ireland. The family moved to Glasgow, Scotland, in 1832, and William studied at Glasgow University and then at Cambridge University in the United Kingdom. He was an active sportsman and enjoyed music, but his main interests were science and mathematics. In 1852, William married Margaret Crum. She died in 1870, and in 1874 William married Fanny Blandy. He was intrigued by the work of James Joule and others, and carried out his own investigations into thermodynamics, collaborating with Joule by letter. Many of his most important contributions to science come from this work. He also acted as adviser to electricity companies and was involved in laying the first transatlantic power cable in 1866. Kelvin died in 1907 and is buried in Westminster Abbey, London.

James Maxwell (1831–1879)

James Maxwell was born in Edinburgh, Scotland. He was the only son of a lawyer. At first, he was taught at home by his mother and then studied at Edinburgh Academy. In 1847, Maxwell went to Edinburgh University to study philosophy, and three years later he moved to Cambridge University, in the United Kingdom, to study mathematics. While at Cambridge, Maxwell published numerous papers about mathematics, light, optics, and astronomy. He became a professor at both Cambridge and London Universities. His main achievements were the kinetic theory of gases and his mathematical proof that light, electricity, and magnetism were all different versions of the same thing. He married Katherine Mary Dewar when he was 27, but they had no children. Maxwell died of cancer in 1879.

Glossary

ampere (amp) unit of electric current

antimatter opposite of matter

cathode negatively charged electrode

Celsius scale scale for measuring temperature, on which water freezes at 0 °C (32 °F) and boils at 100 °C (212 °F)

condense change from gas to liquid

conductor material that electricity can travel through

coulomb (C) unit of electric charge

cyclotron machine that accelerates positively charged particles

diaphragm thin, flexible layer

dynamo machine that generates electricity

electrode conductor through which a current enters or leaves a liquid or gas

electrodynamics study of the movement of electric charges

electromagnet magnet that can be controlled by an electric current

electromagnetism relationship between magnetism and electric currents

electron negatively charged particle in an atom

element material, e.g. oxygen, made up of a single type of atom

evaporate change from a liquid into a gas

filament very fine wire

first law of thermodynamics scientific law that says: however much energy goes into something, the same amount of energy must go out of it

flywheel heavy wheel, attached to a shaft, in a machine

Geiger counter instrument that measures radioactivity

Industrial Revolution period of great expansion of industry that began in England in the 18th century

joule (J) unit of heat

Kelvin scale temperature scale on which the lowest point is -273.15 °C (the coldest any material can be)

kinetic energy energy of anything that is moving

molecule two or more atoms joined together

neutron particle in an atom that has no charge

nuclear fission splitting an atom into smaller particles

nuclear fusion joining atoms together

nucleus central core of an atom

ohm (Ω) unit of electrical resistance

particle accelerator machine that accelerates charged particles

patent legal document that prevents other people copying an invention

piston cylinder that moves back and forth inside an engine

pressure amount of force

proton positively charged particle in an atom

quantum mechanics theory that explains how waves and particles behave

quantum theory idea that energy comes in small amounts called quanta

resistance measure of how difficult it is for electricity to flow through a material

rotor arm that revolves inside a machine or engine

second law of thermodynamics scientific law that says: heat energy will move from a hot place to a cooler place, but not the other way round

Special Theory of Relativity scientific theory that says: the speed of something that is moving can only be measured relative to the speed of something else

spectrum arrangement of rays in order of their wave frequency, wavelength, or the amount of energy they contain

thermodynamics study of heat in relation to other forms of energy

vacuum space that contains absolutely nothing

volt (V) unit of potential electrical difference

voltage energy needed to push an electric charge around a circuit

volume amount of space inside a container

wave mechanics science that uses the Schrödinger equation to explain the behaviour of waves and particles

wave theory theory that explains the principles of wave mechanics

Further resources

If you have enjoyed this book and want to find out more, you can look at the following books and websites.

Books

21st Century Science: Energy
Chris Oxlade
(Franklin Watts, 2004)

Dead Famous: Albert Einstein and his Inflatable Universe
Mike Goldsmith,
Philip Reeve (illustrator)
(Scholastic Hippo, 2001)

Energy Essentials: Nuclear Energy
Steven Chapman
(Raintree, 2005)

Looking at Energy: Nuclear Power
Fiona Reynoldson
(Hodder Wayland, 2005)

*Making Sense of Science:
Electricity and Power*
Peter Riley
(Franklin Watts, 2005)

*Science Files: Electricity
and Magnetism*
Steve Parker
(Heinemann Library, 2004)

Science Files: Heat and Energy
Steve Parker
(Heinemann Library, 2004)

Science Files: Nuclear Energy
Steve Parker
(Heinemann Library, 2004)

*Young Oxford Library of Science:
Energy and Forces*
Neil Ardley
(Oxford University Press, 2002)

Websites

**California Energy Commission
www.energyquest.ca.gov/
index.html**
Activities, games, projects, and information about energy topics, including biographies of famous scientists.

**Institute of Physics,
United Kingdom
www.physics.org**
Site of the UK's Institute of Physics, with information, activities, and games about energy and other physics topics.

**Museum of Science, Miami,
Florida, United States
www.miamisci.org/af/sln**
Discover energy facts and information with the Atoms Family.

**Yahoo Directory
www.yahooligans.yahoo.com/
Science_and_Nature/Physical_
Sciences/Energy**
Information about many aspects of energy science.

**US Government Energy
Information Administration
www.eia.doe.gov/kids**
Energy facts, history, games, and activities.

Index